101 Things I Learned in Advertising School

Other books in the 101 Things I Learned® series

101 Things I Learned in Architecture School (MIT Press)

101 Things I Learned in Business School

101 Things I Learned in Culinary School

101 Things I Learned in Engineering School

101 Things I Learned in Fashion School

101 Things I Learned in Film School

101 Things I Learned in Law School

101 Things I Learned in Urban Design School

101 Things I Learned® in Advertising School

Tracy Arrington with Matthew Frederick

THREE RIVERS PRESS

NEW YORK

Three Rivers Press and the Tugboat design are registered trademarks
of Penguin Random House LLC.

101 Things I Learned is a registered trademark of Matthew Frederick.

Library of Congress Cataloging-in-Publication Data is available upon request.

ISBN 978-0-451-49671-3
Ebook ISBN 978-0-451-49672-0

Printed in China

Illustrations by Matthew Frederick except lessons 15, 25, 29, 40,
45, 48, 55, 57, 69, 73, 74, 75, 76, 77, 81, 83, 91, and 97
Cover illustration by Matthew Frederick

10 9 8 7 6 5 4 3

First Edition

From Tracy
For my miracles Ryan Amelia and Calen Xavier . . .
I love you the most. Don't ever forget.

And in memory of the man who believed
that reading was dreaming with your eyes open.
The mansion, robe, and crown are yours.
I love you . . . a lotta bit.

Author's Note

Advertising is a multibillion-dollar industry that can't stand on its own. It is completely reliant on other businesses. We ad folks say we work in advertising, but we really work in the automotive, film, retail, grocery, telecom, insurance, technology, education, finance, travel, energy, medicine, manufacturing, and hospitality industries.

This hadn't occurred to me when I decided to study advertising. As a math nerd, I hoped to find a niche for my analytical skills in a field more exciting than finance or chemical engineering. This called for me to travel well outside my comfort zone. Other advertising students seemed better suited to the field, with skills in art, writing, photography, psychology, and computer science. But it turned out that all of us had a lot to learn. Advertising requires many types of people, with widely varied skills and areas of focus.

My own skills now extend well beyond data analysis—although not into areas I could have predicted. My knowledge is odd and random. I know how to re-thermalize ground beef. I know why a luxury boutique associate walks you to the restroom, and why you need a load equalizer to upgrade your Jeep's headlights to LEDs. I know why the power in your house is dirty, even though you pay for green energy. I know the recipe for movie theater popcorn.

The somewhat scattershot nature of advertising makes it interesting to ad people, but it may be why it often gets a bad rap. To some, advertising has no soul, no center. It's superficial. It's alternatingly irritating and boring. It's intrusive. It's the art of lying.

The reality is that advertising is more complex than many people think. There are many different skills to bring to it, many ways to enter it, and many things to do when you get there. As for that crack about the art of lying, I would argue the opposite: advertising is the art of telling the truth. An ad campaign succeeds when it brings forward an embedded truth—about the product or service, our needs or idiosyncrasies as consumers, our daily foibles, or the fixations and biases of our culture. An ad campaign resonates when it shows us, at some level, who we are.

I have assembled the following lessons to help you figure out what advertising is and where you might belong in it. You probably will find that the lessons that appeal to you most are different from those favored by a classmate or colleague. And when you read them again in six months or six years, they may mean something very different, as fresh understandings and experiences change what you see in, and learn from, each. Along the way, I hope they will push you out of your comfort zone and give you the grounding, perspective, provocation, and insight to find your own place.

Tracy Arrington

Acknowledgments

Thanks to Sean Adams, Ashley Andy, Diane Heidenwolf Beauchner, Brian Benschoter, Tricia Boczkowski, Tatum Brown, Michelle Cheney, Lisa Dobias, Clark Evans, Sorche Fairbank, John Floeter, Tara Ford, Kirya Francis, Matt Inman, Phil Johnson, Gene Kincaid, Andrea Lau, Rebecca Lieberman, Jill Libersat, Elizabeth McCarthy, the Minions, Jeff Nixon, Amanda Patten, Charlie D. Ray, Janet Reid, Angeline Rodriguez, Molly Stern, and Rick Wolff.

101 Things I Learned in Advertising School

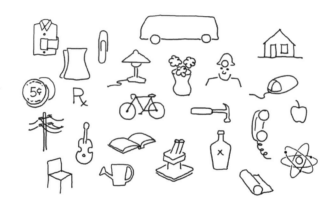

People who dislike advertising should do everything themselves.

When you can buy something made by others for less than it costs to make it yourself, you become a consumer. Modern economies are based on the mass acceptance of this proposition. Each of us specializes and is productive in one or a few areas, and depends on others' specialization and productivity in other areas. Advertising is how we find our way to things others provide. It is a necessary companion to mass production and mass consumption.

art galleries
books
brewing supplies

fitness equipment
brewing supplies
linens

hot tub and pool
fireworks
knitting
surf

vinyl records
framing
golf equipment

fireworks
medical supplies
flea markets
vinyl records
car batteries

The most disproportionately common store type, selected states
Source: *Huffington Post*/Yelp, 2015

A lot of people are like you, but just barely.

The target audience for an ad campaign shares an attribute, interest, or behavior. If you are part of the audience, you might be inclined to create a campaign you feel would appeal to you as a consumer. If you're a manly whiskey aficionado trying to sell whiskey, for example, you might imagine a print campaign in *Maxim,* your favorite magazine. But data reveals the magazine most read by whiskey drinkers is *Better Homes and Gardens*.

Base a campaign on insights into the audience that can be proved by data, not on what you think would work on you or people you know.

Is aware of   Considers   Is interested in   Likes   Prefers   Purchases

Mercury
Plymouth
Saab

The product purchase path

Consumers travel a product purchase path for every buying decision. Each step on the path represents a strengthening of the consumer's tie to the product. For inexpensive items, such as tacos or gum, the path is short and even instantaneous. For expensive or personal items, such as automobiles, washing machines, and engagement rings, the path can extend for months or even years.

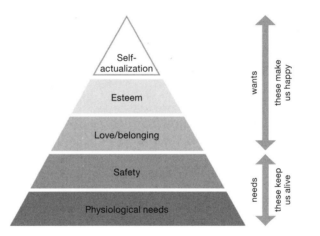

Maslow's hierarchy

Don't start with the product; start with a need or want.

Vegetable juice is a product; nutrients are a need; relief from guilt over a bad diet is a want. Lawn seed is a product; satisfying the homeowner's association is a need; making the neighbors jealous of your lush carpet is a want. Sunblock is a product; avoiding skin cancer is a need; looking younger is a want. A coat is a product; staying warm is a need; maintaining your reputation as a fashion guru is a want. Automobile tires are a product; keeping one's children safe in the car is a need; looking cool on the road is a want.

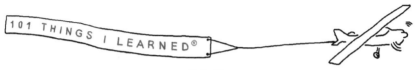

Out-of-home

airborne signage, billboards, branded tchotchkes, taxi and transit signage, experiential events, kiosks, shopping malls, T-shirts, tattoos, and everything outside the other categories

Video	**Audio**	**Digital**	**Print**
any medium with moving images	any listenable medium with no visual component	e-mail, social media, general web advertising	magazines, newspapers, fliers, direct-mail catalogs

The five media categories

Any surface can be an advertising medium—but you shouldn't necessarily use it.

The environment in which an ad is viewed strongly influences the audience's response to the advertised product or service. Advertising a brand to people waiting in line at the Department of Motor Vehicles might lead them to associate it with tedium and regimentation. An ad for an otherwise appealing brand in a public restroom may appear crass and lowbrow. An ad for a funeral home at the gates to a cancer center will be certain to prompt resentment.

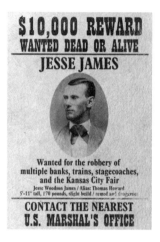

The six elements of a print advertisement

Headline: Communicates a problem or benefit, or provokes curiosity.

Image: The subject of the ad, the product/service offered, the environment in which it will be used, the problem it can solve, or the benefit it will impart.

Body: The main textual portion. It builds interest in the product/service by focusing on key benefits. It may be eliminated if the ad is meant to provoke especially strong emotional association, with the expectation the audience will seek information online.

Call to action (CTA): Encourages the reader, often with a sense of urgency, to take a specific action, e.g., "Visit your dealer today."

Contact information: Tells where to reach the business or how to take advantage of an offer. Traditionally included the company's name, address, and phone number, but now may be limited to a web address or social media identifier.

Company identifier: Usually a logo, but sometimes only the company's name.

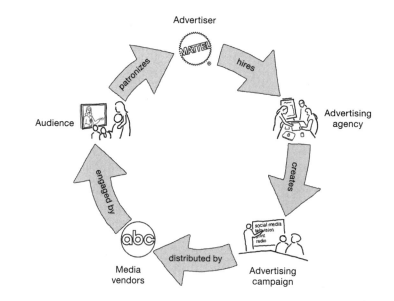

Advertiser

hires

Advertising agency

creates

Advertising campaign

distributed by

Media vendors

engaged by

Audience

patronizes

An advertising agency doesn't advertise.

Advertiser: A person, organization, or company seeking to influence or inform others through mass communication.

Advertising agency: A business hired by advertisers to develop strategies and materials that will drive consumer awareness and action.

Media vendor: A communications outlet, such as a television network, website, newspaper, or billboard owner, that sells time or space for advertisements.

Typography

Imagery

Personality/tone of voice
(Aflac shown)

Color palette

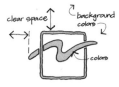
Logo display

Common brand standards

An ad isn't a one-off.

A business or other organization presents itself publicly in many ways. Ideally, each is faithful to a set of **brand standards** that ensure that the personality, look, and feel of the brand are consistent in every venue, from online ads to signage to the answering of phones at the customer call center.

Refer to the advertiser's brand standards before starting an ad campaign. If standards have not been established or are outdated, help the client develop them so you can move forward with a shared understanding of the context for the campaign.

Art is the idea, not the image.

The visual product of an ad campaign should be aesthetically appealing, but the true art of advertising lies in developing intellectual insights into the behavioral, psychological, and cultural context in which a product or service is used.

If your hand skills are poor, you don't have to be a poor artist. Focus on developing insights and on communicating them the best you can. Trace, or cut and paste, images; draw stick figures; carefully select the words that convey your ideas, and evaluate your ideas critically. If you do have strong visual communication skills, don't rush to create something that looks like an ad but lacks insight.

"Great designers seldom make great advertising men, because they get overcome by the beauty of the picture—and forget that merchandise must be sold."

—JAMES RANDOLPH ADAMS

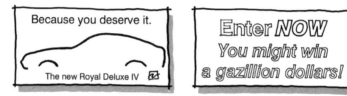

Brand campaign

Direct-response campaign

Brand or direct-response campaign?

Brand, or "soft-sell," campaigns are long-haul, foundational efforts. They build general identity and familiarity by communicating what a company stands for. They are effective in setting quality expectations and establishing an emotional connection with potential buyers. They are most useful in building consumer awareness of brands and products in which the product purchase cycle is long.

Direct-response, or "hard-sell," campaigns are focused efforts that motivate the audience to take a specific action, such as making a phone call, clicking a link, downloading an app, making a purchase, or voting. They are best for accomplishing a specific goal in a limited amount of time, such as selling 100 cars in July. The success of a direct-response campaign is measurable by comparing pre- and post-campaign data.

Sales representatives

Customer service

Branded merchandise

App

Retail environment

Website

Some common touchpoints

Touchpoints

A touchpoint is any aspect of a business with which a consumer interacts. Through touchpoints, consumers develop a holistic impression of a business and its integrity, quality, and product line. Ideally, customers' after-purchase experience with the customer service department is thoroughly consistent with the ad campaign that prompted their awareness of the brand.

Emphasize *reach* when selling toilet paper. Emphasize *frequency* when Beyoncé is coming to town.

Reach is the number of people who hear your message. If a product is used by a wide range of people and without seasonal variation, advertise it to as many people and in as many different venues as possible over a long period of time, even if intermittently.

Frequency is the number of times people hear a message. If your product appeals to a specific audience within a narrow time frame, advertise it with great frequency in the available time span.

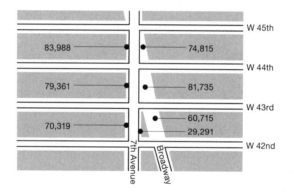

83,988

74,815

W 45th

W 44th

79,361

81,735

W 43rd

70,319

60,715

29,291

W 42nd

7th Avenue

Broadway

February 2017 average daily pedestrian counts, Times Square, New York City
Source: Times Square Alliance

The biggest advertising decision most businesses make is location.

Businesses that value drive-by or walk-in traffic benefit from being in high-traffic areas. But even a company that does not depend on direct customer contact will enjoy the increased brand awareness that comes from having its corporate sign in a busy location. Companies in out-of-the-way locations, or whose interaction with customers is exclusively online, typically must direct any rent savings to advertising.

"Before being a guerrilla, you are my son."

An advertising campaign helped end the world's second-longest civil war.

The Fuerzas Armadas Revolucionarias de Colombia (FARC, the Revolutionary Armed Forces of Colombia) began engaging in terrorist acts against the Colombian government in 1964. After more than 45 years of conflict, the Colombian Ministry of Defense sought the assistance of an advertising agency to discourage revolutionary guerrillas from continuing their involvement.

Shortly before Christmas in 2010, ad agency Lowe SSP3 placed decorated holiday trees in a jungle frequented by FARC fighters. Among them was a banner reading, "If Christmas can come to the jungle, you can come home. Demobilize." Guerrillas were observed defecting, to be with their families for the holidays. A year later, on a river regularly traveled by guerrillas, the agency floated a raft carrying glowing plastic balls, along with gifts and messages from the guerrillas' families. Guerrillas again were observed demobilizing.

FARC announced a unilateral cease-fire a few years later. It has since negotiated an agreement with the Colombian government to end the long dispute.

Don't judge; discern.

Don't view a product positively because it appeals to you, and don't judge it or its audience negatively if you would not use it yourself. Accept and inhabit the point of view, emotional state, and aspirational mind-set of the product's user. If the ad that results from your efforts is not to your or the client's personal liking, remember that the point is to appeal to the target audience, not to yourself or the advertiser.

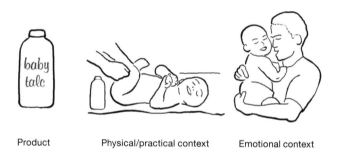

Product   Physical/practical context   Emotional context

17

Demonstrate the context.

Consumers don't buy a product because of the product; they buy it because they want to make their lives better. Featuring the context in which consumers are likely to use a product makes it easier for them to associate personal reward with it.

This product is for
everyone who . . .

This product is for
the person who . . .

You'll reach more by targeting fewer.

No product and no ad campaign will resonate with everyone. Identify and target one person who is predisposed to *get* it—a particular type of individual with an inherent understanding of your product's value. There will be others like him or her. If you try to reach everyone, you risk going unnoticed by your core. It's better to reach a relative few who love your product and will pay for it than to reach a lot more people who are lukewarm about it and won't buy it.

If the core customer is especially hard to identify, learn more about the people who would *never* use the product and whose thoughts you otherwise would be unlikely to seek. Interview them to gain an understanding of who they are. In the gaps, you might find your target audience.

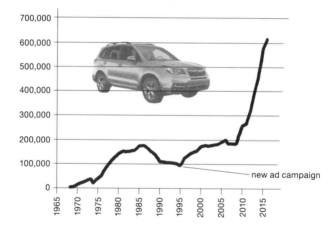

700,000
600,000
500,000
400,000
300,000
200,000
100,000
0

1965 1970 1975 1980 1985 1990 1995 2000 2005 2010 2015

new ad campaign

Subaru of America sales, 1968–2016

Subaru finds its core audience.

After introducing its cars to the United States in 1968, Subaru struggled to build sales and establish a market share comparable to other Asian imports. By the early 1990s, its sales were in decline. Subaru began to accept that it never would be a mainstream brand. But who *did* like Subarus, and why?

Subaru surveyed its customers. It found that half the company's sales were driven by five groups: educators, health-care workers, technology professionals, "outdoorsy" types, and single female heads of household. These customers valued Subaru's all-wheel drive for getting them to work in foul conditions, and that the wagons could haul lots of gear while being more maneuverable than a truck.

Subaru launched an ad campaign targeting all five groups. Among the female household heads, it noted a high proportion of lesbians. Subaru began incorporating coded references in its ads to appeal to gays and lesbians. It sponsored gay pride parades, partnered with the Rainbow credit card, and hired Martina Navratilova, a lesbian former tennis pro, to appear in its ads. The campaign was met by threats of a boycott, but Subaru found that the protestors had never bought one of its cars. The company has been growing ever since. In 2016, Subaru of America set its eighth consecutive annual sales record.

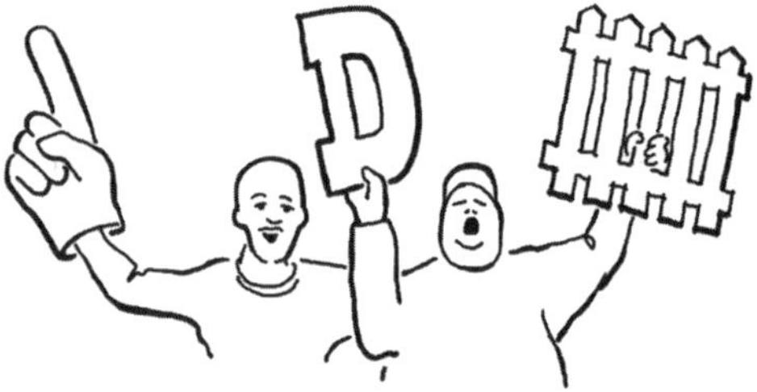
D

Find people who are gaga.

Seek people who *dwell*. When people like something enough to pay for it, they exhibit greater dwell time and higher rates of ad recall. Subscribers of *Jiu-Jitsu* read it cover to cover, for example, but someone handed a copy will not. People who pay for *South Park* on Hulu watch it closely, but others may not notice an episode—or the accompanying advertisements—on regular TV.

Connect with an existing fan base. People take pride in their status as part of a team, whether as sports fans or advocates of cancer awareness. They may spend 3 times more for a mug with a team logo versus a plain mug because of a desire to connect to the team. Aligning a brand with a popular team can maximize its exposure.

Create a fan profile. Every product has a fan base—people who love it, buy it often, and tell others about it. Create a fan profile by identifying dominant demographics and behaviors among existing fans, and target others who act and think similarly.

Find people who are gaga about related things. Look for audiences that are enthusiastic about things related to the product. If you run a doughnut shop, find people who love coffee, morning newspapers, or local businesses.

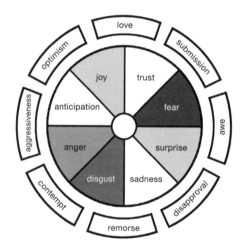

Plutchik's wheel of emotions (partial)

21

The more expensive the product, the more emotional the appeal that must be made.

The value of luxury goods is found typically in their superior quality, but even more so in the emotional satisfaction they provide. By associating pride, joy, accomplishment, exclusivity, and envy with their products, expensive brands enhance their perceived value. The more successful a brand's emotional appeal, the greater the profit margin it can enjoy between production cost and retail price.

22

If you want customers to forfeit their privacy, offer a proportional benefit.

The most useful and accurate data usually comes directly from customers. Most people will provide some personal information if given something in return. They may submit their email address for a coupon, watch a 30-second video for an hour of Wi-Fi, or answer several survey questions to read an article behind a paywall.

Privacy is almost always sacrificed linearly, however. So if you are seeking sensitive information, make sure the "give" is good, or you won't be able to get.

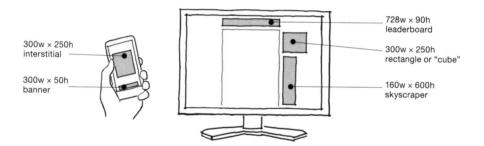

300w × 250h
interstitial

300w × 50h
banner

728w × 90h
leaderboard

300w × 250h
rectangle or "cube"

160w × 600h
skyscraper

Selected standard online ad sizes in pixels, per Interactive Advertising Bureau

23

Let digital audiences decide what works best for them.

In print media, one creates the ad judged most likely to work. In the digital realm, the audience can help figure it out. By producing multiple ads or variations of the same ad, you can learn in real time which performs best by tracking engagements with the ads and the resulting sales. Algorithms can track the performance of different ad sizes, color schemes, fonts, images, copy points, offers, and calls to action, and serve the most appealing formats most often.

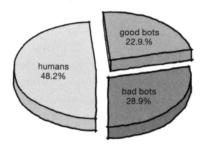

2016 Web traffic
Source: Imperva Incapsula Bot Traffic Report

You'll be lucky to reach half your online audience.

Despite careful targeting using demographic and personal criteria, at least half of online ads are never seen by the target audience due to:

Broken/slow loading: When an ad doesn't load properly or quickly enough, a person might navigate away before seeing it, yet the advertiser may be charged.

Concealment: An ad at the edge of a browser window might be completely hidden, save for a sliver. This may be enough for it to count as viewed.

Pixel stuffing: An ad might be "stuffed" by a dishonest media vendor into a single pixel. It won't be seen by anyone, but will be counted as viewed.

Ad stacking: An ad is placed directly over another ad. The lower, unseen ad will be counted as viewed.

Bot traffic: A "good" bot crawls the web to create legitimate content for search engines. A "bad" bot is software that mimics human browsing behavior—even scrolling and clicking on links—to artificially drive up ad view counts.

Ad blocking: The Interactive Advertising Bureau estimated in 2016 that 26% of desktop users and 15% of mobile consumers used blocking software.

John Wanamaker

"Half the money I spend on advertising is wasted; the trouble is I don't know which half."

—JOHN WANAMAKER, department store magnate

BLADDER
CONTROL
IS CLASSY
518-555-5484
Hudson
www.DrRichardMWood.com

After a billboard in Catskill, New York

Call out the audience only if it's in trouble.

An ad for a bail bondsman can ask if you're being pursued by the law. A loan company or tax attorney can ask if you are in debt. A crisis hotline can wonder aloud if you are having dark thoughts, are being abused, or are struggling with addiction.

But Payless can't say its shoes are for people with very little money. Christian Louboutin can't say his shoes are for people with lots of money. Nine West can't say its shoes are for fashionable women who can't afford Louboutins. They must attract the notice of their target audiences through subtext—their ads' images, colors, fonts, music, and turns of phrase, as well as the actors, models, or spokespersons appearing in them. If the subtext is right, the audience will know it is being addressed. Those who don't get it weren't meant to.

Beacons use GPS technology to send offers to retail shoppers.

It's advertising until it lands in the cart.

Point-of-purchase (POP) displays, shelf hangers, and product packages are physically closer to the consumer than any other form of advertising. They are the "last touch" influences before the consumer decides whether to purchase. They should reinforce the tone and look of the brand that advertising media previously established. A recognizable consistency imparts comfort and moves the shopper closer to purchase.

Unmodulated wave

Frequency modulation (FM)

Amplitude modulation (AM)

Why AM radio sounds lousy

28

Radio waves naturally vary in amplitude (height) and frequency (their rate of "wiggle"). AM broadcasts communicate their sound information through variations in amplitude, while FM uses variations in frequency. The variations are accordingly decoded by AM and FM receivers. But between transmitter and receiver, environmental factors—weather, geographic obstructions, buildings, and other radio signals—intervene. Amplitude is distorted by these factors, but frequency generally is not. Additionally, amplitude deteriorates with distance, while frequency does not. Thus, an AM broadcast rarely can maintain a pure signal, while FM maintains most or all of its quality throughout its effective range.

Even under ideal broadcast conditions, AM sounds inferior. An FM signal has a bandwidth covering nearly the entire range of human hearing. An AM signal's bandwidth is much narrower—wide enough for speech, but not for a full range of musical sounds.

Pure play
available online or
via satellite only

Streaming
terrestrial AM/FM radio
heard via Internet

Terrestrial
traditional tower-based AM
and FM broadcasting

less advertising

more advertising

Commercial radio

29

Use duplication for radio frequency.

People rarely listen to only one radio station. The listeners that different stations share comprise their **duplicated audience.** If a radio campaign needs to reach a lot of people, advertise on stations that have low audience duplication, so many different listeners hear it. If the objective is frequency, choose stations that share a lot of listeners so the same people will hear the message again and again.

	8:00	8:30	9:00	9:30	10:00	10:30	11:00	11:30
HLN	Forensic Files	Forensic Files	Forensic Files	Forensic Files	Forensic Files	Forensic Files	Forensic Files	Forensic Files
HGTV	House Hunters	House Hunters International	House Hunters	House Hunters International	Flip or Flop	Flip or Flop	House Hunters	House Hunters International
abc	Scandal		How to Get Away With Murder		7 News at 10PM	Jimmy Kimmel Live		Nightline

Denver area prime-time listings

Advertise on broadcast TV by program. Advertise on cable TV by network.

30

The ABC, CBS, NBC, and FOX networks were created during the broadcast era of television. Their mission and programming model remain almost identical to what they were originally: each network aims to reach a wide demographic by airing various types of programs for different audiences throughout the day. By contrast, a typical cable television network seeks an audience with a specific interest. It runs the same types of programs every day and repeats episodes frequently.

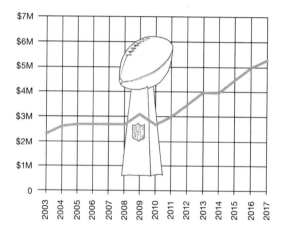

Average cost for 30-second Super Bowl network commercial

Everyone can afford to advertise during the Super Bowl.

31

Television ad time is purchased at either the network level or the local "spot" level. A network-level Super Bowl ad will reach a national audience and will cost several million dollars. At the local level, ads cost much less. A 30-second spot in Amarillo, Texas, is about $3,400; in Presque Isle, Maine, $1,800; and in Juneau, Alaska, $810.

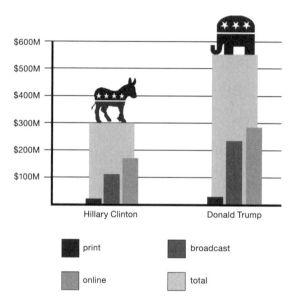

$600M
$500M
$400M
$300M
$200M
$100M

Hillary Clinton   Donald Trump

■ print   ■ broadcast

■ online   ■ total

Free media earned by U.S. presidential candidates, 2016

Don't buy it if you can earn it.

32

Paid media is conventional advertising distributed to the public through media outlets. The cost is determined by the size of the audience that will see the ad and the demand for the space.

Earned media is exposure such as news coverage, editorials, and social media buzz. There is no cost to its subject.

Earned media may be based on a press release distributed by the party seeking exposure—for example, a car company announcing its new models, a department store hiring a new CEO, or a politician declaring candidacy for office. Often, it is reported by media outlets as "straight" news.

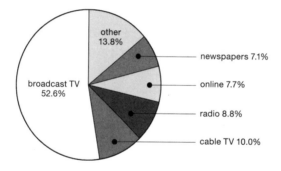

other
13.8%

newspapers 7.1%

broadcast TV
52.6%

online 7.7%

radio 8.8%

cable TV 10.0%

Estimated U.S. political spending by media share, 2016

Politicians pay the least.

33

Broadcasters are required by the Federal Communications Commission to sell time to federal political candidates at their lowest rates for 45 days before primaries and 60 days before general elections. Political action committees (PACs) are not so protected. Stations might even charge them double or triple the normal rate to make up for their reduced earnings.

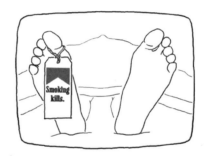

The Fairness Doctrine

The U.S. Federal Radio Commission was created in 1926 to safeguard political dialogue in the new field of radio broadcasting. Among its first mandates was a 1929 declaration that radio stations, when presenting one side of a controversial issue, had to allow the other side to present its position if it so requested.

In 1968, the FRC's successor, the Federal Communications Commission, expanded what became known as the Fairness Doctrine to commercial advertising, by mandating that every TV and radio station airing cigarette ads also had to air public service announcements on the dangers of smoking.

The Fairness Doctrine was dismantled over subsequent decades. However, an **equal-time rule** remains in effect for elections. It specifies that radio and television stations selling airtime to candidates must make similar time available to their political opponents.

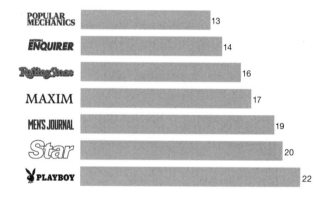

Magazines with most tobacco advertising pages, April–September 2012
Source: Media Radar

The federal ban on cigarette advertising increased smoking.

Cigarette advertising does little to create new smokers; mostly it helps an advertiser recruit existing smokers from other brands. Antismoking public service announcements, on the other hand, have proved effective in discouraging nonsmokers from starting to smoke and in encouraging light smokers to quit.

When the U.S. government prohibited the advertising of cigarettes on TV and radio, starting January 2, 1971, the expectation was that smoking, already in decline, would decrease even more dramatically. Instead, for more than two years after the start of the advertising ban, smoking increased. The major reason was that the advertising ban eliminated the basis for invoking the Fairness Doctrine. With stations forbidden to air cigarette ads, they could no longer be required to air antismoking PSAs. The benefits of the mandatory PSAs were lost.

Jack Palance as Curly, in *City Slickers*

A priority does not include *and.*

A campaign can have several goals but only one priority: to increase sales 10%, raise awareness 30%, or win an election. If a priority contains the word *and,* it has not defined the thing that must take precedence over everything else.

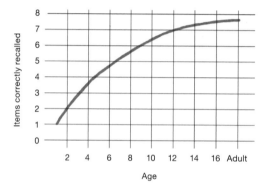

Adult memory can recollect a sequence of about seven numerical digits.

More choices are paralyzing.

In a landmark study, researchers Sheena Iyengar and Mark Lepper set up a table at a food store and displayed 24 varieties of jam. They provided a $1 off coupon to shoppers who tried the free samples provided. On another day, they displayed only six varieties. The smaller display attracted less interest, but motivated sales at a rate ten times that of the larger display.

Psychologists believe that offering too many choices discourages shoppers from buying, for several reasons: it induces anxiety by being time consuming, it encourages shoppers to think they should make a perfect choice, and it asks them to keep track of more items than they naturally can. For similar reasons, menu engineer Gregg Rapp recommends that restaurants present seven or fewer choices per menu category.

Most people pick medium.

38

People don't want to seem cheap, but they also don't want to overspend. When faced with a roster of unfamiliar choices, most people will purchase a product with a middle-tier price—or, at minimum, the second-least-expensive one. For this reason, the next-to-lowest-priced meal and the second-cheapest bottle of wine on a restaurant menu should have the highest profit margin.

Reactance

Our interest in a behavior tends to increase when our freedom to participate in it is limited. In a study of **psychological reactance** (Lessne, 1987), researchers found that an ad for a One Day Only sale increased the likelihood of purchase more than ads for sales of longer or unstated duration. Another study (Lessne and Notarantonio, 1988) found that shoppers purchased more items on average when limited to buying four than with no quantity limit. Reactance also can work in reverse: a high-pressure sales pitch can cause a shopper to shun an item, even if initially interested in it.

Reactance occurs in many other contexts. Our response to time limits may explain the success of the Home Shopping Network, which allows purchases only while a product is featured on air. A study (Mazis, Settle, and Leslie, 1973) found that residents of Miami, where phosphates had been banned, evaluated phosphate-containing laundry detergents more favorably than did residents of Tampa, where they were permitted. And in 2003, entertainer Barbra Streisand sought to protect her privacy by blocking the publication of photographs of her home. Her efforts drew more attention to it. Mike Masnick of Techdirt christened the phenomenon "the Streisand Effect."

39

Aspiration isn't always forward looking.

40

An aspiration is a strong, long-felt desire, yearning, or ambition. It is what we want our lives to *be,* and thus projects us into the future. But we often desire a future more like the past, one that will have the happiness, security, and simplicity we remember, or think we remember, from our childhoods. Look both ways in figuring out how the audience wants to live.

Foie gras $ 21.86
everyday low price

Roasted duck $ 32.98
priced for quick sale

Chicken Salmonella $ 9.88
won't last

Charm them with pricing.

$9.99/$9.95 pricing: Studies suggest, because we read from left to right, that we attach greater importance to the first numbers in a series. We perceive, in effect, $9.99 to be closer to $9 than to $10. This perception may be reinforced when the dollars are rendered larger than the cents, as in $9^{99}.

Oddball pricing: A price of $2.08 or $3.67 suggests the seller is offering an item at the best terms possible. Walmart, which eschews special sales, uses this tactic.

41

Band pricing: Online shoppers may search within a low–high band, e.g., armchairs from $300 to $500 or $500 to $700. Depending on the bands' setup, a $500 chair might not appear in the lower band, while a $499 chair will, meaning it will be seen by more shoppers.

Menu pricing: Restaurants often favor .95 price endings, which perhaps project greater dignity than .99 endings. Whole-dollar prices ($10.00 or $10) suggest the discreet handling of money after a meal, absent the clinking of coins. Menus that omit dollar signs altogether (*"Foie gras* 19") suggest a genteel experience elevated above commercial tawdry. A Cornell University study (Yang, Kimes, and Sessarego, 2009) found this last format increases customer spending over menus that mention dollars—whether with a symbol ($) or written out (*dollars*).

Give the throwaway an afterlife.

Americans throw away 29 million tons of non-biodegradable packaging every year. By investing in sturdy, customized bags and boxes, brands can reduce landfill waste, provide value to the consumer after the sale, and make an advertising impression with each reuse.

A package doesn't have to be as elegant or distinctive as a Tiffany box to be effective. A branded restaurant plastic cup, for which refills are free or inexpensive, will build repeat business while placing the brand in customers' offices, cars, and cupboards. A logo on a cardboard box will increase brand exposure during shipping—and even after, when reused by customers to mail personal items. Consumers will appreciate the additional options while they reduce environmental impact.

42

Here are some
mints for your
bad breath.

Thanks. Here's
a brown sack
for your face.

Guilt 'em.

Sampling a free doughnut from a grocery store tray increases the likelihood you will put some in your cart. Being handed a doughnut by a person makes purchase even more likely, as it invokes your **reciprocity instinct.** The more direct or personal your interaction is with someone who does something for you, the stronger your instinctual response to even the score.

A study published in the *Journal of Applied Social Psychology* (Strohmetz, 2002) tested the effect waiters could have on tipping by bringing mints when delivering checks to their customers. One group of waiters delivered mints without mention, resulting in a tip increase of 3% over a control group. A second group mentioned the mints as they delivered them, producing a 14% higher tip. In a third group, the waiters brought mints with the check, then returned later to deliver more mints while noting aloud that they thought the customers might want more. Tips increased 21%.

The researchers concluded that personalization was the key. Customers perceived the follow-up by the third group of waiters as a post-purchase visit—a demonstration of genuine concern.

43

Wendy's founder and CEO Dave Thomas appeared in over 800 TV commercials, more than any company founder ever.

Modeling the 1% is risky.

Celebrities and other members of the social and economic elite can help increase brand awareness if they share some lifestyle interests with mainstream consumers—even if the common interest is the celebrity's acting, modeling, or music career. But members of the elite with whom the audience shares no evident interests can generate resentment. It's especially risky to feature a company's chief executive officer, whose commonality with the consumer is limited to the brand itself. Unless the CEO is unusually unpretentious and personable, his or her appearance in an ad may look like a grab for the customer's money.

Dove's "Real Beauty" campaign

Dove manufactures beauty products, including soap, deodorant, and shampoo. In 2013, it began to sell the idea that women are more beautiful than they think.

In the video-based campaign, women described themselves as an artist seated behind a curtain created a sketch. Subsequently, a stranger described the same woman as the artist created a second sketch. Each woman was then shown her two portraits. Her own description of a tired, wrinkled face contradicted the stranger's description of a beautiful, vivacious visage.

The campaign was viewed by more than 50 million people within 12 days, becoming the most viral video ad up to that time. It did not mention soap or any other product once.

Traditional advertising
clear distinction between
content and advertisement

Product placement
advertised product
appears within content

Native advertising
presented to resemble
journalistic content

The advertorial

Native advertising appears in an editorial context, such as a general-interest magazine or newsy-looking website. It seeks to camouflage itself as a news article, op-ed, product report, or other editorial content. It doesn't contain a hard-sell message but seeks to provide tips, hints, best practices, or expertise.

An advertorial may be received favorably by visitors to a DIY website or readers of a supermarket tabloid. But in some contexts the audience may feel confused or deceived by the intentions of the publication.

14' × 48' standard billboard

60" TV

Here's
my card.

Where?

2" x 3½"
business card

Don't miniaturize the billboard. Don't magnify the business card.

Different media make different demands upon the advertiser and audience. This requires that you develop a separate approach to each. A billboard is enormous but is viewed fleetingly; even people with the time to read paragraphs of text won't be able to overcome the medium's inherent coarseness. An online video ad, although superficially similar to a TV ad, will be watched from a closer distance on a desktop, tablet, or mobile device—although perhaps for only the first few seconds if there's a "skip" option. Business cards are tiny and may be barely noticed when received, but they are touched directly and can be examined later in complete detail.

47

FEDERAL TRADE COMMISSION
PROTECTING AMERICA'S CONSUMERS

You can stage the truth, but you can't lie.

Demonstrating the actual use of diapers, deodorants, and even drain cleaners can be unpleasant. If you can't show how a product is used without offending, stage it. No one will fault you for a simulation if the alternative is uncouth. Highlighting positives and downplaying negatives is unethical only if it deliberately misrepresents or is an outright lie.

48

The key ingredient in propaganda is truth.

Propaganda promotes a point of view or agenda, typically of a political nature. Its methods are biased, deceptive, exaggeration prone, and confusion inducing, but its central tactic is the deployment of highly accurate truths. The truths are carefully curated or presented out of context, leading the gullible to believe the accompanying distortions and lies are also truthful.

49

Legitimate persuasion seeks to change opinions by demonstrating the greater inherent worth of a position. It presents the various sides of an issue with reasonable completeness and fairness, and aims to show why the arguer's position, on balance, is preferable. Propaganda tends not to change opinions as much as expose and heighten existing opinions.

"All propaganda . . . must fix its intellectual level so as not to be above the heads of the least intellectual of those to whom it is directed. . . . The broad masses of the people are not made up of diplomats or professors of public jurisprudence nor simply of persons who are able to form reasoned judgment in given cases, but a vacillating crowd of human children who are constantly wavering between one idea and another. . . . The great majority of a nation . . . are ruled by sentiment rather than by sober reasoning."

—ADOLF HITLER, *Mein Kampf*

50

© Copyright

Protects written, visual, musical, and other works for the author's life plus 70 to 120 years after death. A company logo, mascot, or similar identifier cannot be copyrighted.

TM ® SM Trademark

Registration (®) with U.S. Patent and Trademark Office protects slogans, sounds, logos, and images identifying the source of goods or services. Non-registered marks are indicated ^{TM} or ^{SM} (service mark).

Intellectual property

Any existing image, music, character, or copy you wish to reuse in an ad is probably protected by copyright or trademark. Permission and payment for reusing a protected asset depends on when, where, how, and how often you intend to use it. A full buyout allows unlimited use. Otherwise, permissions and payment are negotiated for each use. An agreement that allows use of a photo in three newspaper ads in Portland will not allow its use in a magazine in Seattle. Music used in a 60-second radio spot cannot be used in a 30-second version without a new agreement.

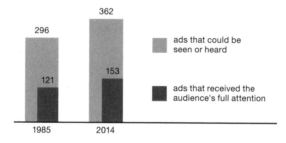

51

296

362

121

153

ads that could be
seen or heard

ads that received the
audience's full attention

1985

2014

Daily advertising exposure per person
Source: Media Dynamics, Inc.

Wearout

All ads eventually lose effectiveness. Running an ad after it has worn out can irritate and anger consumers. Once maximum effectiveness has been reached, the onset of wearout is rapid. The audience won't be won back; once it is over something, it's over it.

Wearout is a function of the interaction of **frequency, exposure,** and **time.** An ad run heavily and targeted to the same audience may reach wearout in four weeks. The same ad run at a moderate frequency for one week a year can be effective for decades. Some Cadbury Crème Egg television ads have been unchanged for more than 30 years. They run only before Easter, when they benefit from audience nostalgia.

52

Sidestep the clutter.

A message can be distinguished from the same-category clutter by placing it in an unexpected yet logical place. If a city tourism department advertises on a travel website or in *Condé Nast Traveler,* for example, it may get lost amid the clutter of its competitors, who also will advertise there. But if the city is known for food and music, it might find a more effective advertising medium in FoodNetwork.com or *Rolling Stone* magazine.

53

After a Converse advertisement

Change the motivation.

When a brand or product is stale and sales are stagnant, find a new way for it to answer to consumers' needs. Kelley Blue Book, publisher of an automobile pricing manual, turned itself into a real-time digital resource for all things cars. Sears, for decades a go-to source for tools and lawn tractors, famously accentuated its softer side, both to advertise its line of women's goods and to acknowledge that women influence the majority of buying decisions. Converse, upon recognizing that more technically advanced products from competitors had superseded its Chuck Taylors as an athletic shoe, repositioned them as a fashion statement.

54

Helen Lansdowne Resor's 1911 ad campaign for
Woodbury Soap is considered the first to use sex successfully.

Don't use sex to sell unsexy things.

If you use sexy imagery in advertising a practical item such as a computer or lawn mower, the audience is almost certain to see through the ruse. They will quickly recognize your transparent attempt to gain their favor and likely will experience psychological reactance against it (Brehm, 1966).

55

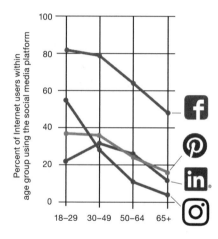

Percent of Internet users within age group using major social media platforms, 2015
Source: Pew Research Center

Meet young audiences on their turf.

In the early 2000s, Old Spice was an aging brand with an old customer base. It hired Wieden+Kennedy to reach out to younger consumers. It launched a 2010 TV ad campaign, "Smell Like a Man, Man," with actor Isaiah Mustafa playing the "Old Spice Guy" with tongue-in-cheek machismo. W+K culled favorable online commentary on the commercials from Facebook and Twitter, and developed a video response campaign. Within a few days, it posted 186 personalized videos on YouTube, with the Old Spice Guy responding directly to fan comments.

Twitter followers, Facebook fans, and subscribers to the brand's YouTube channel increased exponentially as the videos became one of the most popular online interactive advertising campaigns in history. By the end of 2010, Old Spice had become the top-selling men's body wash in the U.S.

56

A 2008 logo for Britain's Office of Government Commerce (OGC)
was pulled after rotation was found to suggest an aroused man.

How many ways can a junior high schooler make fun of it?

Writing an ad is like naming a newborn: wise parents consider how others might ridicule every potential name. Before launching an ad campaign, brainstorm with everyone possible—including people not involved in the campaign—on ways to tweak, distort, or parody your tagline, ad copy, product name, commercial, and logo. Rearrange the words, syllables, and letters. Look at them in different fonts. Brainstorm the meanest, most vulgar, and most inappropriate memes. Mispronounce them. Create unintended rhymes. Sexualize them.

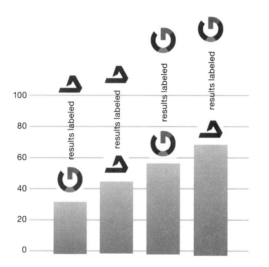

Percentage of respondents preferring search results

Research to discover, not to affirm.

Confirmation bias is our tendency to notice or favorably interpret evidence that supports our preference, and to ignore, discount, or distort that which does not.

A 2013 SurveyMonkey study revealed confirmation bias among users of on-line search engines. Researchers showed a group of consumers search results from Google and Bing, with each set labeled according to its source. A majority preferred the results labeled Google. The researchers then showed a second group results that were deliberately mislabeled. A majority again preferred the results labeled Google, even though they were Bing results. The outcome was attributed to Google's strong brand identity, which led participants to confirm the preference they held prior to the survey.

58

0 1 0 0 0 1 0 1   0 1   0 1 0
1 0 0 1 1 1   0 1 0 0 1 1 1 1
0 1 1   1 0 0 1 0   1 0 1 0 0
0 0 1 0 0 0 1 0 1 0 0 1 0 1 1
1 0 0 1 1 1 0 0 1 1 1   0 1 0
1 1 0 0 1   0 1 1   1 0 0 1 0
0 0 0 1 0 0 0 1 0 1 0 0 0 1 0
0 1 0 0 1 1 1 0 0 1 1 1   0 1
0 1 0 1 1   1 0 0 1 0 1 0 1 0

Datafication

the systematic recording of
information in any form

Digitization

the recording of information in a
binary format for use by a computer

Data

First-party data: Information a company collects directly from a consumer. It may be given voluntarily, as when one gives a home address for an in-store purchase, performs a Google search, or posts on Facebook. Or it may be given involuntarily via tracking cookies placed by a website on a computer to monitor browsing activity.

Second-party data: Consumer information that one company acquires from another company, by purchase or mutual agreement. For example, a luxury car manufacturer purchases data from a luxury watchmaker, or the two companies agree to share their data.

59

Third-party data: Consumer information purchased by an advertiser from a data aggregator, which has collected data from many sources to create a holistic picture of the habits and preferences of a specific person or the user(s) of a particular IP address. The advertiser uses the data to target specific audiences in future advertisements.

Randomer is accurater.

The more randomly a data set is acquired, the more accurate it will be. But randomization doesn't mean winging it; it requires systemization. If you are conducting a political survey at a grocery store, your data will be more random and more accurate if you systematically quiz every tenth person exiting than if you "randomly" approach shoppers, because the latter will be influenced by your preference to talk to some strangers over others.

However, even the most carefully acquired data is not wholly random. Data gathered from grocery shoppers may be distorted by the store brand, the location, the fact that it's a grocery store and not a farmer's market or co-op, and the day or hour the survey is taken. Online surveys are distorted by the fact that those who take them are inclined to click a link. Up and down votes on YouTube are distorted because viewers are predisposed to like the videos they seek out.

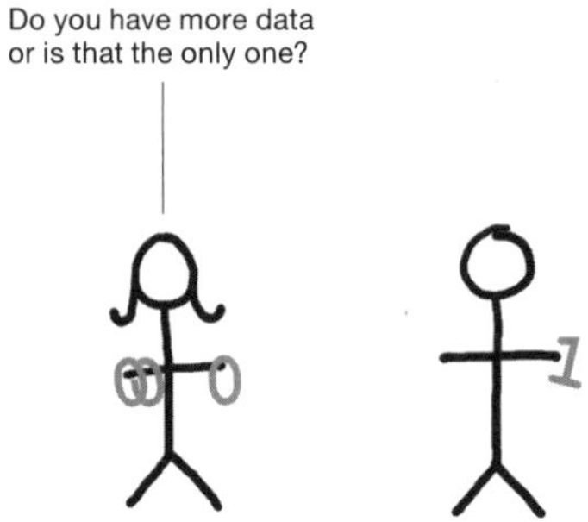
Do you have more data
or is that the only one?

60

Data is singular enough.

Most nouns are **counting nouns;** they have singular and plural forms. Lenore has one bicycle, three dollars, and many friends. A **mass noun** is never pluralized: luggage, transportation, health. A **collective noun** similarly refers to a group as a single entity: class, flock, audience. However, it may be singular or plural, depending on whether it refers to the group or its members: "The jury is sequestered"; "The jury are divided in their opinions."

Data is the plural of *datum,* a single piece of information. It appears to be a counting noun, which would lead one to say, "The data are reliable." However, the relationship of *data* to *datum* is almost nonexistent in ordinary use. *Datum* is most often used to mean a reference point. *Data* acts as a mass noun.

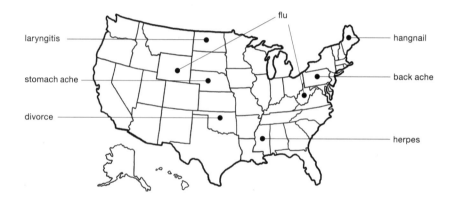

laryngitis

flu

hangnail

stomach ache

back ache

divorce

herpes

Which state had the highest ratio of the search term relative to all search terms?
Source: Google Trends, 2016

Two views of big data

Big data trumps expertise. Before the digital era, experts relied on their experience, intellect, and intuition to explain human behavior. Big data makes such expertise unnecessary. It tells Walmart that bad weather causes a run on strawberry Pop-Tarts and that geographic concentrations of Google search items can point to locations of pending disease outbreaks—things no expert would think to look for. In the digital era, experts aren't smarter than data; they read it for what it has to say.

Big intuition trumps big data. Data tells us who we have been, not who we can be. True innovation results through impulses that we feel, not information that we read. Highly innovative firms like Apple and Tesla do little to no market research. True genius intuits, not deduces, the way forward.

62

"If I had asked people what they wanted, they would have said faster horses."

—HENRY FORD

Sometimes screwing around is screwing around. Sometimes it's actual work.

Students arrive at advertising school with different skills, strengths, and weaknesses. If you have an analytical or linear orientation, you may be puzzled by students who approach problem solving obliquely—and who might look like they waste too much time. But if you have to create a campaign for Dave & Buster's, can you learn what you need to know through web research or analyzing data? Or is there value in hanging out at Dave & Buster's? And while you're at it, why not visit Buffalo Wild Wings and a local arcade for comparison?

64

Being creative by yourself doesn't work.

A good idea isn't a good idea in isolation; it connects with people in the real world. If the process of creating doesn't include social engagement, the result is unlikely to engage anyone except you.

When you're struggling to come up with ideas, working with others can get you unstuck. Even if they give you no specific ideas, they'll point you in some directions you hadn't considered. And if you disagree with their suggestions, you probably will become motivated to come up with new ideas, if for no other reason than to show you know better than they do.

65

You don't have to defend one idea to the death.

Having an idea negatively criticized can leave you feeling misunderstood. You might feel you are too creative to be appreciated, that being a genius means being resented by the masses. You might cling more tightly to the idea others have said won't work and refuse to move on to new ideas.

But even if those who shot down your brilliant idea misunderstood it, why should you be unable to move on? If you really are creative, you are capable of an infinite number of brilliant ideas. Holding tightly to one prevents the flow of others.

66

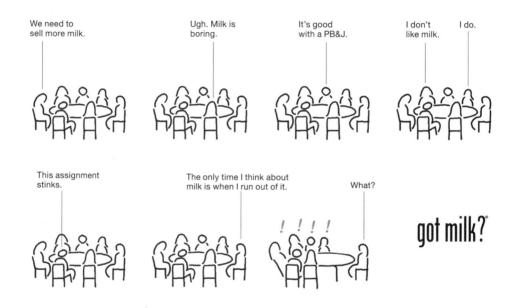

After the advertising campaign by Goodby, Silverstein & Partners
for the California Milk Processor Board, 1993

Insight on insight

An insight is not an observation or invention. It isn't a flash of inspiration or the pinpointing of a missing ingredient. It is the realizing of the essence of a situation.

The search for insight can be tedious and deflating. It requires researching, brainstorming, focusing, refocusing, sifting, resifting, doing, undoing, and often giving up in frustration. But in giving up, one becomes a stranger to his or her situation and may be open to a fresh perspective on it.

When it is eventually found, an insight will be both broad and specific: it will reveal a human truth or cultural-scale experience, yet will connect concretely to the product or product category. It will surprise, inspire, and provide clarity. It will feel like something you had not thought of before yet were aware of all along.

The truest truth

Before trying to write a clever tagline or ad copy, square up to the reality of the brand. What is the most direct, unfiltered truth you can think of that describes it, its customers, the public's view of it, or *your* view of it?

The truest truth is a short statement, usually with a *but* or other qualifier, that captures your distinction between those who do and don't embrace the brand, or the internal dialogue you imagine a potential buyer engaging in. For example:

BMW: They piss off other drivers, but that's kind of the point.

Crest: I don't know if it's better or worse than Colgate, but I'm used to it and my teeth haven't fallen out.

Smartfood: It's probably *not* smart . . . or is it? Is it healthy? Well, it tastes good.

You might come up with more than one truest truth for a brand. Whatever it is, it won't become a tagline or ad copy. But it will help center the campaign on the reality of the brand and steer you away from saying only what you think you should say.

America's Most Exciting Bank™

A tagline doesn't have to tell the whole truth, but it should tell a believable truth.

Back claims with evidence. If you say your customer service is responsive, the audience has no reason to believe you. If you say, "We'll respond within an hour," you provide the audience with believable, testable evidence.

Make a *distinguishing* claim, not a superlative claim. If you say you make the most advanced products, have the most integrity, or build to the highest quality standards, should the audience believe you? Superlatives invite skepticism. Saying how you are different, rather than better, may be more effective in gaining interest.

Don't make a claim if a reasonable person would not assert the opposite. A BP ad boasts, "It's our best fuel ever." But no fuel company would advertise, "Our new gas isn't as good as our old gas," making BP's claim meaningless to the consumer.

69

Don't make a claim because it makes you feel good about yourself. Does a rural, regional bank really believe its customers seek banking excitement? Does it benefit by suggesting all of America is its target market?

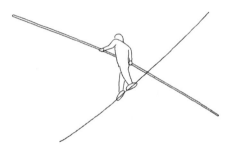

If you're being truthful, it will feel risky.

If you create an ad that is based on what you think it is supposed to do or copy an ad used by a successful brand, your ad will become part of the clutter. If you want to be perceived as different, you have to *be* different. In order to be different, you have to start fresh. You have to risk being naïve. Only then can you honestly see who the audience is, what its needs are, and how to reach it. Solve the problem before you in the most truthful way, and you will end up with the most appropriate, original solution.

70

"Cut the marketing bullshit and get to the truth."

—JOHN C. JAY, in the documentary *Briefly*

71

Bro, I don't think dependability belongs in that list.

Dude, I don't think manscaping belongs on any list. Let's get to the *breastaurant*.

Breastaurant is a registered trademark of Bikinis Sports Bar & Grill.

Everyday words come from advertising.

Because of advertising, you can use a *crayon* to create a *circular* for a *shopportunity* on *Frisbees,* and tape a *Xerox* of it to an *elevator* door. If the elevator's *dependability* is in question, take the *escalator* to meet your *framily* for lunch, where you can compare the *drinkability* of *uncolas.* Before going out, however, you might lower your *zipper* and do some *manscaping.* Remedy any blunders with a *Kleenex, Band-Aids,* and *aspirin.*

72

JUST DO IT.

Adapt emerging language.

Nike's famous slogan, created by the Wieden+Kennedy agency in 1988, was inspired by "Let's do it," the last words of murderer Gary Gilmore at his 1977 execution. But its long-term success may be due more to its kinship with "do it," a euphemism for sex. The phrase was more risqué in 1988 than it is today, but it lay within popular awareness. Wieden adapted the phrase to the brand: *Just* ties Nike to immediate action, a sensibility suited to athletic gear. The concluding period affirms the slogan as a positive directive to the wannabe athlete. Throughout the long life of the slogan, Nike has not used direct sexual inference in its ads.

MetLife

Old saws still cut wood.

Make the person viewing the ad want to be in the ad. Create a world or lifestyle in which customers can imagine themselves enjoying an experience, engaging friends, or solving a problem.

Look forward, not backward. Show the audience that the product can be instrumental in leading them into the future.

Sell the positive. It's OK to point out the negatives of an experience, but get the audience excited about how the product can get them through it.

You can sell a young person's car to an old person, but not an old person's car to a young person. Most people want to imagine themselves younger; an ad should help them do this.

A good advertisement is the worst thing that can happen to a bad product. If a campaign is better than the product, the bad news will become widely known.

Puppies and kids can sell almost anything. Unimaginative, but often true.

This is not your father's Oldsmobile.

The campaign that helped shutter America's oldest carmaker

Oldsmobile, founded by Ransom E. Olds in 1897, enjoyed a distinct identity and solid sales through much of the 20th century. But after reaching a peak of 1.1 million units in 1985, it faced an abrupt decrease in buyer interest due to an aging model lineup, shifting demographics, and competition from foreign carmakers.

In 1988, Oldsmobile introduced an ad campaign meant to alter the perception of its cars. Unfortunately, "This is not your father's Oldsmobile" did not resonate with car shoppers. Postmortems faulted the campaign for selling what an Oldsmobile was not rather than what it *was,* and for looking backward rather than forward. The campaign left Oldsmobile in a no-man's-land: it told existing Olds owners they were old-fashioned, while it cautioned young shoppers against buying an old person's car. Oldsmobile had alienated its existing customers without attracting new ones.

The company replaced the failed tagline in 1990, but the tepid "We have got a brand new Oldsmobile" also failed to inspire. By 2000, sales were at 25% of their mid-80s peak, and parent corporation General Motors decided to terminate the brand. The last Oldsmobile was built in 2004.

Snap, Crackle, and Pop, the mascots of Kellogg's Rice Krispies

Three is good company.

Ideas and images presented in threes are naturally enjoyable, interesting, and memorable. Life, liberty, and the pursuit of happiness. *Planes, Trains, and Automobiles. Veni, vidi, vici.*

Three is the minimum number of entities that creates a pattern or rhythm. If you have four, consider cutting one. If you have two, keep working on it.

76

Think different.

eat fresh.™

Write good.

A slogan or tagline doesn't have to be grammatically correct. But if you use incorrect grammar, make sure it's short and catchy.

77

S-E-N-S-A-Y-...

Spell sensationally.

A **sensational spelling** is a deliberate misspelling of a word to draw attention to it, for example Flickr or Krispy Kreme. Compared to a conventional spelling, a sensational spelling may be more memorable and easier to procure as a domain name.

Sensational spellings are often more trademarkable; if conventional spellings were regularly permitted to be trademarked, public use of ordinary language would be limited. The Syfy cable TV network changed its name from Sci-Fi in 2009 for this reason. The sensational spelling of the Froot Loops trademark brings its owner, the Kellogg Company, an additional benefit: protection from charges of false advertising, as the breakfast cereal contains no fruit.

78

Rhetorical communication
usually hierarchical, with one person "in the know"; aims to alter opinions or motivate action

Relational communication
tends to be non-hierarchical and inclusive; aims to strengthen connections among discussants

The more you talk, the less you will be trusted.

Coworkers who brag at length about their accomplishments will often seem suspect. Kids and spouses who offer detailed explanations for why they are late can raise more concerns than they relieve. Acquaintances who corner others at a cocktail party with windy arguments on why their advice should be followed can raise eyebrows. Long explanations make people uncomfortable.

79

Clichés bog down creativity.

It's better to express your thoughts in clumsy, original words than to use overly familiar language or well-practiced buzzwords. When you contribute clichés to the creative process, you sidestep your truest ideas and opinions. Your rough thoughts are far more useful, as they motivate others to fill in the gaps and smooth the rough spots you create. Clichés put buttons on the creative process, which others must undo before they can move it forward again.

80

only
the ball
should
bounce.

Anna Kournikova, in ad for the Multiway Sports Bra by
Britain's Shock Absorber Inc.

No padding.

Too much information can overwhelm the reader and render a message ineffective. It can suggest the writer has presumed the audience's interest or doesn't trust the customer to "get" it. It also might suggest that the originator does not understand the core of his or her message.

When editing for length, be ruthless. But don't simply shorten your message; uncover its essence. Cross out all words but the most operative. If you feel there is more to say, run multiple ads or drive consumers to a website. In doing so, simply give the web address rather than state, "Please visit our website at www.101ThingsILearned.com for more information."

After a McDonald's advertising campaign

Seven words on a billboard.

Billboards are big, but cars drive fast and attention spans are limited. In large media, skip the toll-free phone numbers, wordy explanations, web addresses, and other clutter.

82

"I'm sorry I wrote you such a long letter;
I didn't have time to write a short one."

—BLAISE PASCAL, *Provincial Letters,* 1656

83

Lite 'n' Breezee

24-hour pads

Firckmeyer

Security Systems

German tradition. American brewed.

Font is tone of voice.

The font in which a message is presented is itself a form of communication. Lay out your ad copy in many different fonts, including ones far from what you expect to use, to see how it affects the message. A font thought too whimsical may reveal that you can be less serious than you had planned. A slender font might bring unexpected freshness. Italics may bring the quality of a parenthetical whisper or the urgency of motion. An exotic font may suggest exclusivity or handcrafting. You'll know you have found the right font when it doesn't feel like a selection but simply what had to be.

84

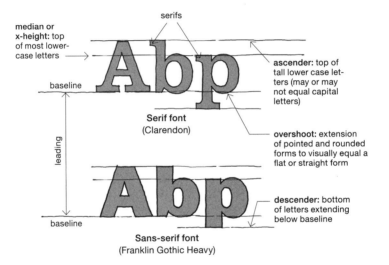

median or
x-height: top
of most lower-
case letters →

serifs

ascender: top of
tall lower case let-
ters (may or may
not equal capital
letters)

baseline

Serif font
(Clarendon)

overshoot: extension
of pointed and rounded
forms to visually equal a
flat or straight form

leading

descender: bottom
of letters extending
below baseline

baseline

Sans-serif font
(Franklin Gothic Heavy)

Sans serif fonts are grotesque.

Historically, all fonts had small embellishments, or serifs, at the ends of each stroke. Their derivation is unclear; they may have served originally to tidy up the edges of letters carved into stone.

When sans serif fonts appeared in the 1700s, some observers found them clumsy and deemed them "grotesque." The moniker became formally attached to many, such as Franklin Grotesque and Monotype Grotesque. The disparagement was perhaps fair: many of the fonts were poorly proportioned and even lacked a lower case. But it was found that sans serif fonts could be read more easily and quickly, suiting them to headlines, billboards, and other simple announcements. Alas, this furthered the opinion that sans serif fonts were crass. A worthy message, detractors held, is delivered with serifs. It is for similar reasons today that the body text in most books, newspapers, and intellectual periodicals and websites is rendered with serifs, even when titles and headings are sans serif. Too, horizontal serifs promote visual cohesion among the letters of a word, easing the reading of running text.

85

Google

1999

Google

2015

Serif fonts don't scale well.

The subtle details of serif fonts are often distorted when rendered on the small screens of mobile devices. Largely for this reason, Google changed from a serif to a sans serif font in 2015, when searches on mobile devices first exceeded searches on desktops. The new font maintains the multicolored playfulness of the original Google font but is more easily read at all sizes.

86

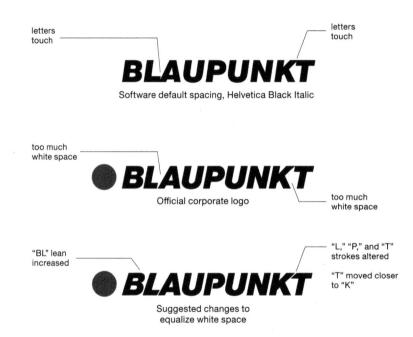

letters
touch

letters
touch

BLAUPUNKT

Software default spacing, Helvetica Black Italic

too much
white space

BLAUPUNKT

Official corporate logo

too much
white space

"BL" lean
increased

"L," "P," and "T"
strokes altered

"T" moved closer
to "K"

BLAUPUNKT

Suggested changes to
equalize white space

Be better than the software.

A font is designed to work in ostensibly every letter combination, but spacing problems can arise. Although they may not be noticeable in ordinary body text, they can become jarring when text is fully justified, enlarged, bolded, italicized, or rendered in an unusual font.

To identify spacing problems, soften your gaze and consider the words as an abstract composition of shapes. Tune in to the distribution of white space, noting where it is disproportionate. If the overall spacing needs adjustment, it can be increased or decreased globally by changing **tracking.** Local spacing between two letters is adjusted by **kerning.** If the text is especially prominent or iconic, as in a logo, the letters themselves might need revision to promote cohesion and balance.

87

Energy oriented
toward the spine

Figure oriented toward
the call to action

Direct the flow of energy.

Arrange figures and objects to call attention to an ad's message. People, animals, and objects usually should face or be inflected toward the body text or call to action. If in motion, they usually should be moving "into" the ad.

If the placement of the ad on a web page is known, its energy usually should be directed toward the center of the screen. In a print publication such as a magazine or catalog, energy is best directed toward the spine. People or vehicles moving away from the spine may appear disinterested, as if they are "leaving" the publication, although this can be less problematic on right-hand pages, where movement to the right matches the direction one's eye and attention are usually headed.

As our brain processes images 60,000 times faster than words, we seek out imagery to shortcut the additional work that words require. If a headline needs to be read before one can make sense of an image, place and size the headline so the eye goes to it first.

We "see" from top to bottom, left to right.

In the West, we tend to view images in the same manner that we read: our eye usually starts at the upper left. For this reason, vehicles shown in profile often face to the left. This allows us to "read" their shape from front to rear.

Make images right-handed.

Studies indicate that viewers respond more favorably to ads depicting a product in a position in which they can readily imagine interacting with it. In one study (Elder and Krishna, 2012), participants viewed advertisements for a mug with the handle oriented in various positions. They were most likely to purchase the mug after viewing an advertisement with the mug handle to the right, a position that suits the hand dominance of about 90% of people.

The colors of iconic brands are easy to recall.

Emote with color.

Black: authoritative, powerful, mysterious, chic

White: pure, clean, innocent, straightforward

Brown: earthy, solid, steadfast, sincere, predictable

Green: natural, fertile, renewable, moneyed, envious

Blue: peaceful, calm, stable, conservative, responsible, sad

Red: passionate, important, dangerous, active, angry

Orange: healthy, energetic, earthy, dangerous

Yellow: happy, cheerful, cowardly, cheap

Purple: creative, imaginative, royal, romantic

[black in
center]

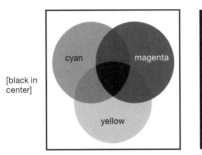

cyan

magenta

yellow

CMYK

use when selecting and
specifying colors for
printed material

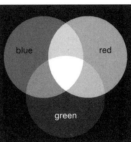

[white in
center]

blue

red

green

RGB

use when selecting and
specifying colors for
web publication

Include some black.

Nearly every color scheme benefits from some black, which helps anchor a composition to a page and guards against its looking faded or poorly printed.

Spring: Pale yellow-green, light blue, and pink, with splashes of stronger color. Suggests newness, youth, gentleness, femininity.

Summer: Emphasizes primary (red, yellow, blue), secondary (orange, green, purple), and tertiary colors. Suggests simplicity, action, straightforwardness.

Autumn: Brown, olive, gold, russet. Suggests maturity, wisdom, earthiness.

Winter: Silver, gray, black. Suggests machinery, coolness, inorganic material.

High-contrast: Black and white, alone or with strong colors. Suggests power, action, decisiveness.

Neon: Hot pink, electric orange, brilliant lime. Suggests fun, youth, sexiness.

Complementary: Based on two colors lying opposite on the color wheel, e.g., blue and orange, red and green, or yellow and purple. Suggests balance.

Monochromatic: Uses colors that are adjacent on the color wheel, e.g., red, yellow, orange; two blues and a teal. Imparts calm.

soft background focus

liquid dish soap for foam

acrylic ice cubes

add water to dark liquids
so light shines through

natural or diffuse
artificial light; no flash

evenly spaced sesame seeds

LTO iced for crispness; place
lettuce ruffle side out; secure to
bun with mini toothpicks

cold burger, slightly larger than
bun; add grill lines with electric
charcoal lighter; brush on
vegetable oil for juiciness

Fuzz it like a pro.

One quality consistently distinguishes professional photographs from amateur photos: depth-of-field (DOF) management. A quality camera allows adjustment of the lens aperture, so the subject of a photo can be placed in sharp focus while the background and foreground are blurred. If your cell phone camera lacks adjustment, you can convincingly fudge background DOF with photo-imaging software.

1   Open the photo in the imaging program. Make a copy of it as a separate layer within the file.

2   The bottom photo will be the background. "Blur" or "soften" the entire image.

3   On the top/subject photo, erase everything but the subject, allowing the blurred background to show through. You usually can achieve a satisfactory result by erasing close to but not quite touching the subject.

4   Evaluate the combined image. You probably will need to further blur the background or adjust the brightness/contrast of one or both layers to adequately emphasize the subject.

10 slides maximum   20 minutes or less   30-point font minimum

Business consultant Guy Kawasaki's 10-20-30 rule

When preparing a presentation, prepare two presentations.

Keep the **room presentation** as brief as possible but long enough to establish your presence as an expert. If you use slides or other visual aids, have very few words on them. Don't read from your visual material, and don't present or talk about every detail. Any areas of confusion can be elaborated on during open discussion.

Create a **leave-behind.** It should cover the same major points as the room presentation but be more robust, with details, charts, case studies, research sources, and appendices. Distribute the leave-behind at the end of your talk. If you hand it out earlier in the hope of having the audience follow you, they will go at their pace instead of your pace. Alternatively, send the leave-behind the following day with a note of thanks.

94

Don't translate criticism literally.

Critics of your work may offer suggestions for remedying its shortcomings. But it's more important to heed their criticisms than their fixes, as one critic might suggest a different fix than another, and all of their antidotes might take you in the wrong direction. But if more than one person comments on the same problem, there's almost certainly a problem.

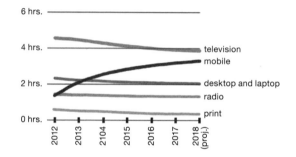

95

6 hrs. ————————————————————

4 hrs. ————————————————— television

————————————— mobile

2 hrs. — ———————————— desktop and laptop

———————————— radio

0 hrs. —■—————■——■——————■——■——————■—— print

2012 2013 2104 2015 2016 2017 2018
                                      (proj.)

Total media time per day, U.S. adults
Source: eMarketer.com

You won't have a healthy relationship if you do all the talking.

Brand communication was once **One to Many.** An advertiser spoke to many consumers with little or no communication in the other direction. Consumers had limited ability to influence brands, their products, and how companies advertised.

In the digital environment, brand communication can be **Many to One.** Consumers can offer their appreciation, annoyance, encouragement, and suggestions directly to brands. If they don't like what they hear or don't feel they are being listened to, the proliferation of media outlets and the ease of access mean they can and will go elsewhere.

96

Volkswagen advertisement featuring 7'1" Wilt Chamberlain, 1966

Admitting flaws elevates credibility.

Volkswagen introduced the Beetle to America in an era of big-car dominance. Rather than take on the big-car makers directly, ad agency Doyle Dane Bernbach decided to celebrate the simple honesty it saw in VW's vehicles. It used unglamorous black-and-white photos rather than the stylized drawings favored by most carmakers, and a copy style that was direct, conversational, and ironic.

Speaking to consumer concerns that a car priced under $2,000 would be of poor quality, DDB offered the headline "Lemon." The ad explained that the pictured car looked like every other Beetle, but a production inspector had found a flaw and sent it back. "We pluck the *lemons,* you get the *plums,*" concluded the ad. An ad for VW's homely Microbus crowed, "Somebody actually stole one." The copy bragged of the engine's dependability and efficiency, claiming it would get a thief farther than any police car.

Reader surveys at the time scored the ads higher than the editorial content in many of the magazines in which they appeared. In 1999, *Advertising Age* declared "Think Small" the number one ad campaign of all time.

97

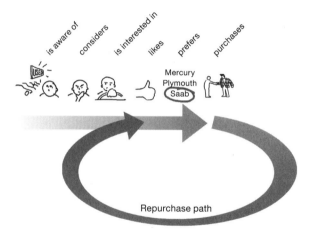

Make the relationship outlast the purchase.

Advertise to existing customers. Consumers want to feel good about their purchase and to know the brand continues to offer desirable products or services.

Provide updates. Offer behind-the-scenes views into company goings-on and products in development, to foster an image of a company that is active and forward looking, and that will offer value when customers next need it.

Cultivate members. Loyalty programs, referral incentives, and inducements for customers to advertise by word of mouth foster an ongoing connection to the brand.

Send a thank-you note following a sale. Customize with the customer's name. Include additional information or incentives for future purchases or referrals.

Prioritize customer service. Problems are inevitable, so anticipate and resolve them sympathetically and thoroughly.

Don't be a pest. Adapt the method and frequency of contact to the product. Make it easy for customers to customize their contact preferences.

"People will forget what you said, people will forget what you did, but people will never forget how you made them feel."

—MAYA ANGELOU

Creative **Specialized** Focused Strategic Leadership Passionate Expert Excellent Experienced Certified

The most frequently used buzzwords in LinkedIn profiles, 2017

What you can do next matters more than what you've done.

Interviewers don't want to see every project you have ever done; they want to figure out if you will fit into their company. Include in your portfolio only your strongest work, and that which suits their needs. If you fail to edit, you will convey exactly that—that you don't know how to edit, and that you might not be sure which work is your best.

Use your portfolio as a vehicle for conversation. Tell the story of projects that capture the interviewers' interest. Relate the problem assigned, your process and insights, how your solution met the client's needs, and even how you could have done a better job.

100

Don Draper, played by Jon Hamm, in *Mad Men*

Seeing your work in an ad is like being a little famous.

As a student, your work is subject to critique by peers, instructors, and industry professionals visiting the classroom. As a professional, it will be critiqued by *everyone*. Your failures will be public. But there's no room to be debilitated by criticism or embarrassment. Your successes will be public, too.

Notes

Lesson 39: Greg J. Lessne, "The Impact of Advertised Sale Duration on Consumer Preference," *Proceedings of the 1987 Academy of Marketing Science Annual Conference;* Greg J. Lessne and Elaine M. Notarantonio, "Effects of limits in retail advertisements: A reactance theory perspective," *Psychology and Marketing* 5, no. 1 (Spring 1988): 33–34; M. B. Mazis, R. B. Settle, and D. C. Leslie, "Elimination of phosphate detergents and psychological reactance," *Journal of Marketing Research* 10 (1973): 390–95.

Lesson 41: S. S. Yang, S. E. Kimes, and M. M. Sessarego, "$ or dollars: Effects of menu-price formats on restaurant checks," *Cornell Hospitality Report* 9, no. 8 (2009): 6–11.

Lesson 43: David B. Strohmetz, Bruce Rind, Reed Fisher, and Michael Lynn, "Sweetening the Till: The Use of Candy to Increase Restaurant Tipping," *Journal of Applied Social Psychology* 32 (2002): 300–309.

Lesson 55: Jack W. Brehm, *A Theory of Psychological Reactance* (New York: Academic Press, Inc., 1966).

Lesson 90: Ryan S. Elder and Aradhna Krishna, "The 'Visual Depiction Effect' in Advertising: Facilitating Embodied Mental Simulation Through Product Orientation," *Journal of Consumer Research* 38, no. 6 (April 2012).

Index

1%, the, 44

Adams, James Randolph, 10
advertiser, defined, 7
Advertising Age, 97
advertising agency
    Doyle Dane Bernbach, 97
    Goodby, Silverstein &
        Partners, 67
    Lowe SSP3, 15
    role, 7
    Wieden+Kennedy, 56, 73
advertising campaigns
    "Got Milk?," 67
    "Real Beauty," 45
    "Smell Like a Man, Man,"
        56
    "Think Small," 97
advertising exposure, 52
advertorial, 46
Angelou, Maya, 99
Apple, 77
audience
    aging, 56
    aspirational mind-set, 16,
        40, 74
    emotional state, 16
    online, 24

targeting, 2, 13, 16, 18, 19,
    20, 21, 26, 30, 40, 53,
    56, 74, 90
young, 56

Band-Aids, 72
beacons, 27
Berkshire Bank, 69
Better Homes and Gardens, 2
Bikinis Sports Bar & Grill, 72
billboards, 47, 82
Bing search engine, 58
Blaupunkt, 87
Bloomingdale's, 42, 43
BMW, 68
bots, 24
BP corporation, 69
brand
    campaign, 11
    emotional appeal, 21
    identity, 54, 56, 58
    standards, 8
Briefly (documentary), 71
Buffalo Wild Wings, 64
business
    card, 47
    location, 14
buzzwords, *see* clichés

Cadbury Crème Egg, 52
California Milk Processor
    Board, 67
call to action, 6, 88
celebrity endorsers, 44
CEO, in ads, 44
Chamberlain, Wilt, 97
choices, ideal number of, 37, 38
cigarette advertising, 34, 35
clichés, 80, 100
Clinton, Hillary, 32
clutter, 53
Coca-Cola, 91
Colombia, government, 15
color, 91, 92
communication, 96
    brevity, 79, 81, 82, 83
    credibility/trust, 69, 97
    grammar, 77
    language, 72, 73, 76, 77, 78,
        79, 80, 81, 82, 83, 84
    rhetorical vs. relational, 79
    subtext, 26
    visual, *see* visual
        communication and
        composition
Condé Nast Traveler, 53
confirmation bias, 58

Converse, 54
Cornell University, 41
cost, *see* pricing
creative process, 9, 64, 65, 66, 67, 68, 70, 80
Crest, 68
customer relationship, 12, 98, 99

data, 2, 22, 59, 60, 61, 62
Dave & Buster's, 64
digital advertising, 23, 24, 47
direct-response (hard-sell) campaign, 11
Dunkin' Donuts, 16
dwell time, 20

earned media, 32
elements of a print advertisement, 6

Facebook, 56, 59, 91
Fairness Doctrine, 34, 35
fans, 20
Federal Communications Commission, 33, 34
Federal Trade Commission, 48
Flickr, 78
fonts, *see* typography
Ford, Henry, 63
fraud, 24
frequency
    of advertisements, 13, 29
    radio broadcasting, 28

Frisbee, 72
Froot Loops, 78
Fuerzas Armadas Revolucionarias de Colombia (FARC), 15

General Motors, 75
Gilmore, Gary, 73
Google, 58, 59, 62, 86
Gund, 77

Hamm, Jon, 101
Hitler, Adolf, 50
Home Depot, The, 91
Home Shopping Network, 39

Instagram, 56
intellectual property, 51
Interactive Advertising Bureau, 23, 24

Jay, John C., 71

Kawasaki, Guy, 94
Kelley Blue Book, 54
Kellogg Company, 76, 78
Kleenex, 72
Kournikova, Anna, 81
Krispy Kreme, 78

limited time/quantity sales, 39
LinkedIn, 56, 100
Louboutin, Christian, 26
luxury goods, 21

Mad Men (television show), 101
MarthaStewart.com, 53
Maslow's hierarchy, 4
Masnick, Mike, 39
mass consumption and production, 1
Maxim, 2, 35
McDonald's, 82
media
    categories, 5
    exposure, 96
    vendors, 7
Mein Kampf, 50
memory, *see* recollection
Men's Journal, 35
MetLife, 74
mobile devices, 23, 27, 47, 86
Mustafa, Isaiah, 56

National Enquirer, 35
native advertising, 46
Navratilova, Martina, 19
needs, vs. wants, 4
Nike, 73
Nine West, 26

Office of Government Commerce (Britain), 57
Old Spice, 56
Oldsmobile, 75
out-of-home, 5

parody, 57
Pascal, Blaise, 83

Payless, 26
Pepperidge Farm, 40
photography, 93
Pinterest, 56
Planes, Trains, and Auto-
        mobiles (film), 76
Playboy, 35
Plutchik's wheel of emotions, 21
point-of-purchase, 27
political advertising, 32, 33, 34
Pop-Tarts, 62
Popular Mechanics, 35
presentation, 18, 66, 94, 95, 100
pricing
        ads, 31, 32, 33
        dollar signs, use of, 41
        earned vs. paid media, 32
        product, 38, 41
        restaurant, 38, 41
priority, identifying, 36
privacy, customer, 22
product
        demonstration/staging, 48
        packaging, 42
        physical and emotional
                context, 17
        placement, 46
        purchase path, 3
        repurchase path, 98
propaganda, 49, 50
psychological reactance, 39, 55

radio, 28, 29
Rapp, Gregg, 37

reach, 13, 29
reciprocity instinct, 43
recollection, 37
repositioning, 54, 56
research, 2, 58, 60, 64
Resor, Helen Lansdowne, 55
restaurants
        menus, 37, 38, 41
        pricing, 38, 41
        tipping of waiters, 43
Rolling Stone, 35, 53

Sears, 54
sex, 55
Shock Absorber Inc. (Brit-
        ain), 81
Smartfood, 68
Snap, Crackle, and Pop
        (Kellogg characters), 76
spelling, sensational, 78
Star magazine, 35
Starbucks, 16, 91
Streisand Effect, 39
Subaru, 19
Subway, 77
Super Bowl, 31
SurveyMonkey, 58
Syfy network, 78

tagline, 69, 77
Techdirt, 39
television, 30, 47
Thomas, Dave, 44
Tiffany & Company, 91

Times Square (New York
        City), 14
touchpoints, 12; *see also*
        customer relationship
troubleshooting, 57
Trump, Donald, 32
truth, 48, 49, 68, 69, 70, 71
Twitter, 56
typography, 84, 85, 86, 87

United Parcel Service (UPS), 91

video advertising, 5, 45, 47, 56
visual communication and
        composition, 9, 84, 85,
        86, 87, 88, 89, 90, 91, 92,
        93, 94
Volkswagen, 97

Walmart, 62
Wanamaker, John, 25
wants, vs. needs, 4
waste, in ad campaigns, 24, 25
Wayne's World (film), 46
wearout, 52
Wendy's, 44
Woodbury Soap, 55

Xerox, 72

YouTube, 56, 60

Tracy Arrington is the Director of Consumer Insights and Media at a full-service advertising agency in Austin, Texas. She has developed advertising and media campaigns for many of the world's leading brands, including AT&T, Bank of America, BMW, Dell, DreamWorks, MasterCard, Nike, Sylvania, Taco Bell, and Walmart. She teaches at the University of Texas at Austin.

Matthew Frederick is an architect, urban designer, instructor of design and writing, and the creator of the acclaimed 101 Things I Learned series. He lives in New York's Hudson Valley.

www.101ThingsILearned.com